TRIVQUIZ

PEOPLE & PLACES

BRIAN WILLIAMS

A GRISEWOOD & DEMPSEY LTD BOOK

This edition published in 1991 by Blitz Editions, an imprint
of Bookmart Limited, Registered Number 2372865.
Trading as Bookmart Limited, Desford Road, Enderby,
Leicester LE5 5AD.

© Grisewood & Dempsey Ltd, 1991

ISBN 1 85605 047 5

Illustrated by Talk Back International Ltd. London.

Printed in Italy

INTRODUCTION

We think that you will find TRIVQUIZ People & Places as much fun to use as it was to compile. The 1,080 questions and answers included in the book should tax your memory, furrow your brow and even make you chuckle or groan. None of them falls within the dusty definition of trivia as 'the humdrum, ordinary or commonplace'. People & Places covers Old Testament prophets, assassinated American presidents and Chinese feats of engineering, as well as shedding new light on some familiar British landmarks and historical figures.

This book is easy to use. The questions come in groups of ten, with each group concentrating on one aspect of people and places, such as Europe, Inventors, Film and TV, or Story Tellers. Questions always appear on a right-hand page and you just turn the page to find the answers. You then move on to the next page for another group of ten questions. When you reach the group numbered 27 you will be at the end of the book (page 60). Then it's back to the beginning for number 28 (and eventually, numbers 55 and 82).

The questions and answers make an interesting read on their own, but it's more fun to turn them into a game. Take it in turns to read the questions or form teams. Win or lose, you'll find it fun, and if you're playing in the car, the motorway miles will slip by unnoticed.

Finally, we should issue a warning: trivia is addictive. By the time you reach the 1,080th answer you'll probably be hooked, and ready for more questions. Don't worry. Help is at hand — in the form of this book's companion volume, TRIVQUIZ General Knowledge.

1 PEOPLE

1 Who was murdered in Canterbury Cathedral in 1170?
2 Whom did Robin Givens marry in February 1988?
3 Which school did Winston Churchill attend?
4 Who is the new Archbishop of Canterbury?
5 Who was the Roman god of wine?
6 How did missionary John Williams die in 1839?
7 What did Richard Byrd do in 1926?
8 Who is said to have introduced the potato to England?
9 Who is the patron saint of France?
10 By whom was St Patrick captured when he was 16?

28 WHO WERE THEY?

1 Who was Gladys Aylward?
2 Who was Balzac?
3 What did Auguste Bartholdi design?
4 What does John Regis do?
5 Who was the Lady of the Lamp?
6 What happened to Sarah Bernhardt in 1915?
7 What did Stavros Niarchos own?
8 Who was Aristotle Onassis' last wife?
9 Who is John Schlesinger?
10 Who was Ed Murrow?

55 ROYALTY

1 Which member of the royal family was born on 1 July 1961?
2 By what name was Edward VIII known to his family?
3 Which king was murdered in the New Forest?
4 Which king called his son 'the greatest ass in the world'?
5 Which king fell in love with Mrs Fitzherbert?
6 How old was Edward VII when he became king?
7 Where did Queen Victoria die?
8 Where was Richard II murdered?
9 Which king was nicknamed 'Crookback'?
10 What relation was Elizabeth I to Henry VIII?

82 AFRICA

1 Which is the largest country in Africa?
2 What is the capital of Kenya?
3 Which country of Africa has the most people?
4 Which is the northernmost African country?
5 Which is the largest island of Africa?
6 Which is the biggest desert in Africa?
7 Where is the Namib desert?
8 What is the chief language used in Cote d'Ivoire?
9 Where is Casablanca?
10 On which river is Khartoum?

A

1

1   Thomas à Becket
2   Mike Tyson
3   Harrow
4   George Carey
5   Bacchhus
6   He was eaten by cannibals
7   He flew over the North Pole
8   Sir Walter Raleigh
9   St Denis
10 Pirates

28

1   A Missionary
2   A French novelist
3   The Statue of Liberty
4   He is a sprinter
5   Florence Nightingale
6   She lost a leg
7   Ships (and other things)
8   Jackie Kennedy
9   A film director
10 US broadcaster

55

1   Princess of Wales
2   David
3   William Rufus
4   George II
5   George IV
6   59
7   Osborne, Isle of Wight
8   Pontefract Castle
9   Richard III
10 Daughter

82

1   Sudan
2   Nairobi
3   Nigeria
4   Tunisia
5   Madagascar
6   Sahara
7   Southwest Africa
8   French
9   Morocco
10 Nile

2 PEOPLE

1 Who was Britain's youngest prime minister?
2 Gertrude Ederle was the first woman to do what in 1926?
3 When did Margaret Thatcher become prime minister?
4 Which famous ballerina died in February 1991?
5 Whose first hit record was 'Heartbreak Hotel'?
6 Of which country is Brian Mulroney prime minister?
7 What is Douglas Hurd's second name?
8 Who is the subject of the world's longest biography?
9 Who is the world's best-selling crime writer?
10 What part has William Roache played on TV since 1960?

29 WHO WERE THEY?

1 What is Rupert Murdoch's first name?
2 What did Arthur Murray teach?
3 What is John Major's wife's name?
4 Who was Audie Murphy?
5 Who was Erwin Rommel?
6 Who is Wole Soyinka?
7 Who was Roger Maris?
8 What did Mark Spitz do best?
9 Who was Alfred Russel Wallace?
10 What did Marcel Dassault make?

56 ROYALTY

1 Which king literally burst from his coffin?
2 Which king was known as the Lionheart?
3 Which monarch was born at 17 Bruton Street, London?
4 What did Elizabeth I nearly die of in 1562?
5 Who married Princess Mary of Teck?
6 Who was the first Hanoverian king of England?
7 Who was the first king of England and Scotland?
8 Who was Charles II's father?
9 How many children did Queen Anne have?
10 How many of them became adults?

83 AFRICA

1 Which country has the initials C.A.R.?
2 What was Zimbabwe's former name?
3 What name did the Gold Coast adopt?
4 On which river is the Kariba Dam?
5 What is Swahili?
6 Which country did Idi Amin rule?
7 Which is Africa's biggest city?
8 What is the capital of Ethiopia?
9 Which country do the Masai come from?
10 What kind of feature are Atlas and Ruwenzori?

A

2

1 William Pitt the Younger (aged 24)
2 Swim the Channel
3 1979
4 Margot Fonteyn
5 Elvis Presley
6 Canada
7 Richard
8 Winston Churchill
9 Agatha Christie
10 Ken Barlow in *Coronation Street*

29

1 Keith
2 Dancing
3 Norma
4 A US soldier turned film actor
5 A German WW2 general
6 A Nigerian writer
7 An American baseball star
8 Swim
9 A naturalist
10 Aeroplanes

56

1 William I
2 Richard I
3 The present Queen
4 Smallpox
5 George IV
6 George I
7 James I
8 Charles I
9 17
10 None

83

1 Central African Republic
2 Rhodesia
3 Ghana
4 Zambezi
5 A language
6 Uganda
7 Cairo
8 Addis Ababa
9 Kenya
10 Mountain ranges

3   *PEOPLE*

1   Who were Shakespeare's 'star-crossed lovers'?
2   Where did Chay Blyth sail in 1970-71?
3   What relation was Queen Victoria to King William IV?
4   Who was known as the Mahatma or Great Soul?
5   What reform did Elizabeth Fry work for?
6   Who painted the Laughing Cavalier?
7   Where was Haile Selassie emperor?
8   What did Hipparchus measure over 2,000 years ago?
9   How did Nero die?
10   What did Sheraton design?

30   *WHO WERE THEY?*

1   What newspaper does Max Hastings edit?
2   What sport does David Seaman play?
3   What does Michael Fish do on TV?
4   Who is Emma Nicholson?
5   What kind of books does Delia Smith write?
6   Who is Jimmy Knapp?
7   Who was Augustus John?
8   What was Barry John's sport?
9   What does Jonathan Palmer drive?
10   What does Norman Painting do on radio?

57   *ROYALTY*

1   Who was Mary II's husband?
2   Which king married Caroline of Anspach?
3   When were the Queen and Prince Philip married?
4   Which of the Queen's children was born in 1960?
5   Which king is said to have burnt the cakes?
6   What was the Queen Mother's family name?
7   Where was the Prince of Wales married?
8   Who was Prince Charles's best man?
9   What is the Princess of Wales's family name?
10   Who was Prince Albert of Saxe-Coburg and Gotha?

84   *AFRICA*

1   In which country is Afrikaans spoken?
2   What is the capital of Zambia?
3   Where do the Yoruba and Ibo people live?
4   Which country has money called naira?
5   Which country has Maputo as its capital?
6   Freed American slaves founded which country in 1822?
7   Which states are Guinea-Bissau's neighbours?
8   In which country is the Aswan Dam?
9   Where is Mount Cameroun?
10   What is the capital of Algeria?

A

3

1 Romeo and Juliet
2 Round the world, east-west, solo
3 His niece
4 Gandhi
5 Prison reform
6 Frans Hals
7 Ethiopia
8 The size of the Moon
9 He killed himself
10 Furniture

30

1 *Daily Telegraph*
2 Football
3 Presents weather forecasts
4 A Tory MP
5 Cookery
6 The leader of the Rail union
7 A painter
8 Rugby union
9 Racing cars
10 Plays Phil in *The Archers*

57

1 William III
2 George II
3 1947
4 Andrew
5 Alfred the Great
6 Bowes-Lyon
7 St Paul's Cathedral
8 He didn't have one
9 Spenser
10 Queen Victoria's husband

84

1 South Africa
2 Lusaka
3 Nigeria
4 Nigeria
5 Mozambique
6 Liberia
7 Guinea and Senegal
8 Egypt
9 Cameroun
10 Algeria

4   *PEOPLE*

1 Where was Daniel Boone born?
2 Who founded the Salvation Army?
3 What year did John Lennon die?
4 What is soccer star Maradona's first name?
5 Who painted *The Birth of Venus*?
6 Who was the first king of Italy?
7 How old was Prince Albert when he died in 1861?
8 Who was Pancho Villa?
9 Who was Ricardo Villa?
10 Where did Leif Ericsson sail?

31   *COUNTRY ASSOCIATIONS*

1 The composer Rossini?
2 The composer Elgar?
3 The composer Wagner?
4 The poet W.B. Yeats?
5 The poet Dylan Thomas?
6 The comedian Billy Connolly?
7 The cricketer Martin Crowe?
8 The philosopher Confucius?
9 The soldiers called samurai?
10 The politician Rajiv Gandhi?

58   *UNITED STATES*

1 Which state is known as the Land of Lincoln?
2 In which state is Cape Canaveral?
3 In which state is Cape Cod?
4 Which state has the nene as its state bird?
5 Which state has Richmond as its state capital?
6 Which city is known as the Windy City?
7 In which state is Pearl Harbor?
8 In which city do the Lakers basketball team play?
9 Where is the Kimbell Art Museum?
10 Which state is known as the Empire State?

85   *SHOW PEOPLE*

1 Which screen comic was nicknamed 'Old Stoneface'?
2 What did Burt Lancaster do in the circus?
3 Stan Laurel was British: true or false?
4 When did Steve McQueen die?
5 Who played the Thin Man on screen?
6 Who was Norman Jean Baker?
7 Did Tarzan ever say 'Me Tarzan, you Jane'?
8 Who swashbuckled in *The Thief of Baghdad* (1924)?
9 Where was Sidney Poitier born?
10 What is Kris Kristofferson's real name?

4

1 Pennsylvania, USA
2 William Booth
3 1980
4 Diego
5 Botticelli
6 Victor Emmanuel I
7 42
8 A Mexican revolutionary
9 An Argentine soccer star
10 North America

31

1 Italy
2 England
3 Germany
4 Ireland
5 Wales
6 Scotland
7 New Zealand
8 China
9 Japan
10 India

58

1 Illinois
2 Florida
3 Massachusetts
4 Hawaii
5 Virginia
6 Chicago
7 Hawaii
8 Los Angeles
9 Fort Worth
10 New York

85

1 Buster Keaton
2 Acrobat
3 True
4 1983
5 William Powell
6 Marilyn Monroe
7 No
8 Douglas Fairbanks Sr
9 Miami, Florida
10 Apparently it is his real name

5   PEOPLE

1 Who composed *The Four Seasons*?
2 What did the Rosenbergs do?
3 Where did Marco Polo start his travels?
4 To whom was Carole Lombard married when she died?
5 Where was Pablo Picasso born?
6 Who is the patron saint of doctors?
7 Who sentenced Jesus to death?
8 What did John Loudon McAdam improve?
9 Was there a real-life King of Scotland called Macbeth?
10 Who was Virgil?

32   COUNTRY ASSOCIATIONS

1 The golfer Severiano Ballesteros?
2 Madeira wine?
3 Edam cheese?
4 The city of Budapest?
5 The city of Lahore?
6 The city of Oslo?
7 The sport sumo wrestling?
8 The singer Joan Sutherland?
9 The runner Kip Keino?
10 The climber Edmund Hillary?

59   UNITED STATES

1 Which is the smallest state?
2 Which state has the same name as a Soviet republic?
3 Where is the Imperial Valley?
4 Where are the iron-rich Mesabi Mountains?
5 Where is Monument Valley?
6 Where is Mount Whitney?
7 Where is the Mount St Helens volcano?
8 Where is the hottest place in the United States?
9 Where is the city of Pittsburgh?
10 Which is the leading wheat-growing state?

86   SHOW PEOPLE

1 Which Fifties singer had a hit with 'Rawhide'?
2 Who created 'Tubular Bells' in 1973?
3 Who starred as the first stage phantom of the opera?
4 By what name is Frances Gumm better known?
5 Where was Hazel O'Connor born?
6 Where was Richard Burton born?
7 Were Ingmar and Ingrid Bergman married?
8 Who played Ashley Wilkes in *Gone with the Wind*?
9 What epic film did Abel Gance direct?
10 Which star of silent films was known as the 'It' girl?

A

5

1. Vivaldi
2. They were spies
3. Venice
4. Clark Gable
5. Spain
6. St Luke
7. Pontius Pilate
8. Roads
9. Yes, he died in 1057
10. A Roman writer

32

1. Spain
2. Portugal
3. Holland
4. Hungary
5. Pakistan
6. Norway
7. Japan
8. Australia
9. Kenya
10. New Zealand

59

1. Rhode Island
2. Georgia
3. California
4. Minnesota
5. Arizona
6. California
7. Washington
8. Death Valley, California
9. Pennsylvania
10. Kansas

86

1. Frankie Laine
2. Mike Oldfield
3. Michael Crawford
4. Judy Garland
5. Coventry
6. Wales
7. No
8. Leslie Howard
9. *Napoleon*
10. Clara Bow

6   *PEOPLE*

1 What did Suzanne Lenglen play?
2 Which Beatles were born in 1940?
3 Who was Jorge Luis Borges?
4 What did Ferdinand de Lesseps build?
5 Where was novelist Doris Lessing born?
6 What nationality is Thor Heyerdahl?
7 Who wrote *The Mayor of Casterbridge*?
8 Who discovered that blood circulates round the body?
9 Who was Shakespeare's wife?
10 What was Mrs Siddons' profession?

33   *COUNTRY ASSOCIATIONS*

1 The statesman Willy Brandt?
2 The traitor Vidkun Quisling?
3 The film director Eisenstein?
4 The comedian Jacques Tati?
5 The Superbowl?
6 Marsala wine?
7 Aztec ruins?
8 The veldt?
9 The 'bullet train'?
10 Ice hockey star Bobby Hull?

60   *UNITED STATES*

1 Which state grows the most cotton?
2 Where is the biggest US oil reserve?
3 Which state has 53 peaks over 4,200 metres high?
4 Where is the Bitterroot National Forest?
5 Which state borders California to the north?
6 In which state is Seattle?
7 Where is the Shenandoah Valley?
8 Where is Oklahoma City?
9 Where is Phoenix?
10 Where is Mt Mitchell?

87   *SHOW PEOPLE*

1 Of which duo is Neil Tennant half?
2 Who is Richard Wayne Penniman?
3 When were Status Quo formed?
4 Who is Richard Starkey?
5 Who were the stars of *All the President's Men*?
6 Where did Celia Johnson have her brief encounter?
7 Are Steeleye Span and Steely Dan the same band?
8 Who made a 1983 album called *White Shoes*?
9 What was the Rolling Stones' first UK hit?
10 Who is John Henry Deutschendorf Jr?

A

6

1. Tennis
2. John Lennon, Ringo Starr
3. An Argentine writer
4. The Suez Canal
5. Iran
6. Norwegian
7. Thomas Hardy
8. William Harvey
9. Anne Hathaway
10. Actress

33

1. Germany
2. Norway
3. Russia
4. France
5. United States
6. Sicily
7. Mexico
8. South Africa
9. Japan
10. Canada

60

1. Texas
2. Alaska
3. Colorado
4. Montana
5. Oregon
6. Washington
7. Virginia
8. Oklahoma
9. Arizona
10. North Carolina

87

1. Pet Shop Boys
2. Little Richard
3. 1967
4. Ringo Starr
5. Robert Redford, Dustin Hoffman
6. A railway station buffet
7. No
8. Emmylou Harris
9. 'I Wanna Be Your Man' (1963)
10. John Denver

7   *PEOPLE*

1 What did Igor Sikorsky build?
2 Who wrote *The Wealth of Nations*?
3 Which country was led by Ian Smith?
4 Which town was represented by Cyril Smith MP?
5 What nationality was Jan Smuts?
6 Who was India's first prime minister?
7 What did Nelson lose in 1797?
8 Who was the last great Aztec emperor?
9 Who was the first Viscount of Alamein?
10 Who was Marianne Moore?

34   *FILMS AND TV*

1 In what year was Robert de Niro born?
2 Who was Liza Minelli's mother?
3 Which actress died in the shower in *Pyscho*?
4 Who directed *Psycho*?
5 Who wrote the words for the musical *Oklahoma*!?
6 In which country was Anthony Quinn born?
7 Who played M in the first Bond film?
8 Who was the human star of *Who Framed Roger Rabbit*?
9 Who played Captain Hornblower on screen?
10 Who starred as Captain Blood?

61   *UNITED STATES*

1 What did bootleggers do?
2 Which US president bought Louisiana from France?
3 What is Cher's real name?
4 Who was Michael Dukakis' running mate in 1988?
5 Who flies in Air Force One?
6 Who commanded US forces in the Gulf War?
7 What is Michael Dukakis' middle name?
8 For what is Geoffrey Beene famous?
9 In which sport did Michael Jordan become famous?
10 What did Susan Blow found in the 1870s?

88   *PEOPLE*

1 Who wrote the jazz piece 'Blue Monk'?
2 What did Mies van der Rohe design?
3 What name did Dino Crocetti croon under?
4 What nationality was singer John McCormack?
5 Where was Liberace born?
6 Whom did Nadezhda Krupskaya marry in 1898?
7 For which county does Graham Gooch play cricket?
8 In which Olympics did Olga Korbut star?
9 Which US designer became famous for jeans ads?
10 Which country does Kenneth Kaunda lead?

A

7

1 Helicopters
2 Adam Smith
3 Rhodesia
4 Rochdale
5 South African
6 Nehru
7 His right arm
8 Montezuma
9 Montgomery
10 An American poet

34

1 1945
2 Judy Garland
3 Janet Leigh
4 Alfred Hitchcock
5 Oscar Hammerstein II
6 Mexico
7 Bernard Lee
8 Bob Hoskins
9 Gregory Peck
10 Errol Flynn

61

1 Smuggle liquor
2 Thomas Jefferson
3 Cherilyn Sarkisian
4 Lloyd Bentsen
5 The President
6 General Norman Schwarzkopf
7 Stanley
8 Fashion design
9 Basketball
10 US kindergarten movement

88

1 Thelonius Monk
2 Buildings
3 Dean Martin
4 Irish
5 Wisconsin, USA
6 Lenin
7 Essex
8 1972 (Munich)
9 Calvin Klein
10 Zambia

8   PEOPLE

1 Who invented morse code?
2 What year did Mozart die?
3 Who was King John's father?
4 Who was John the Baptist's father?
5 What did Karol Wojtyla become in 1978?
6 What did Amy Johnson set records for?
7 What country did Eamon de Valera lead?
8 Where was Charles Dickens born?
9 Who was Sir Robert Menzies?
10 To whom was Nadezhda Krupskaya married?

35   FILMS AND TV

1 Which Western hero was played by William Boyd?
2 What was John Wayne's real name?
3 Who starred in the 1967 Western *Hombre*?
4 Where was Bob Hope born?
5 Who played the rape victim in *Accused*?
6 Which cartoon character eats spinach for strength?
7 What do the initials MGM stand for?
8 Who played Hawkeye in *M*A*S*H*?
9 Name two of the Marx brothers (other than Groucho).
10 What was Basil Fawlty's wife's name?

62   UNITED STATES

1 Did Davy Crockett ever sit in the US Congress?
2 What was Frank Lloyd Wright's profession?
3 What did Orville and Wilbur Wright do in 1903?
4 Who was the first president of the United States?
5 Which US writer wrote the play *Death of a Salesman*?
6 Who wrote the words and music of *Guys and Dolls*?
7 Which American statesman flew a kite in a storm?
8 Which religious group founded Plymouth Colony?
9 What did Francis Scott Key write in 1814?
10 Who commanded the Southern armies in the Civil War?

89   PEOPLE

1 Who played Hans Christian Andersen on film?
2 Who was the first black world heavyweight boxing champion?
3 What year was Glenda Jackson born?
4 In which industry did Lee Iacocca rise and fall?
5 What did Harry Ferguson do in 1909?
6 What nationality was Lester Pearson?
7 Who wrote the music for *Zorba the Greek*?
8 Who is Kylie Tennant?
9 Who was the last tsar of Russia?
10 Whom did Vincente Minnelli marry in 1945?

A

8

1 Samuel Morse
2 1791
3 Henry II
4 Zacharias
5 Pope John Paul II
6 Solo long-distance flying
7 Ireland
8 Portsmouth
9 Australian premier and statesman
10 Lenin

35

1 Hopalong Cassidy
2 Marion Morrison
3 Paul Newman
4 Eltham in England
5 Jodie Foster
6 Popeye
7 Metro Goldwyn Mayer
8 Alan Alda
9 Zeppo, Chico, Harpo, Gummo
10 Sybil

62

1 Yes
2 Architect
3 Flew an aeroplane
4 George Washington
5 Arthur Miller
6 Frank Loesser
7 Benjamin Franklin
8 The Puritans
9 'The Star Spangled Banner'
10 Robert E Lee

89

1 Danny Kaye
2 Jack Johnson
3 1936
4 Car industry
5 Flew the first plane across Ireland
6 Canadian
7 Mikis Theodorakis
8 An Australian novelist
9 Nicholas II
10 Judy Garland

9   PEOPLE

1   What did Ransom Eli Olds do?
2   Who was Il Duce?
3   Who wrote *Utopia*?
4   Who said 'Take away that Bauble'?
5   Who competed in the 'bore wars' of palaeontology?
6   Who was Bloody Mary?
7   Who was Singapore's first prime minister?
8   Who were Russia's Mr B and Mr K in the 1950s?
9   Which Bohemian reformer was burned to death in 1415?
10   What did Lieutenant Lucas R.N. receive in 1856?

36   FILMS AND TV

1   Who is Clark Kent?
2   Who commands the starship *Enterprise*?
3   What is the name of the pub in *Coronation Street*?
4   Who played Mary Poppins on screen?
5   Who directed the 1939 Western *Stagecoach*?
6   Which battle was portrayed in the film *Zulu*?
7   Who played Douglas Bader in *Reach for the Sky*?
8   Who directed the 1948 film *Bicycle Thieves*?
9   Which was the first *Star Wars* film?
10   Who played Han Solo in the *Star Wars* films?

63   UNITED STATES

1   Which general became President in 1869?
2   Who starred in the 1927 talkie *The Jazz Singer*?
3   Who brought in the New Deal in the 1930s?
4   What was President Eisenhower's first name?
5   Who succeeded Richard Nixon as President?
6   Which black civil rights leader was murdered in 1968?
7   After whom was Pittsburgh named?
8   Which US President won the Nobel Peace Prize in 1906?
9   Who was the first American in space?
10   Which American declared that 'history is bunk'?

90   PEOPLE

1   Who invented 'dynamic tension'?
2   What do the initials of W.H. Auden stand for?
3   Who was the first European to sail to India?
4   Who won a 1991 Golden Raspberry for worst actress?
5   Which MP is known as the Beast of Bolsover?
6   Who left an unfinished opera called *Zaide*?
7   For which football clubs did Kenny Dalglish play?
8   Which jazz singer was known as Lady Day?
9   How did Australian premier Harold Holt die in 1967?
10   What is Jimmy Connors' middle name?

A

9

1 Built motor cars
2 Benito Mussolini
3 Thomas Moore
4 Oliver Cromwell
5 Othniel Marsh and Edward Cope
6 Mary I
7 Lee Kuan Yew
8 Bulganin and Khruschev
9 John Huss
10 The first Victoria Cross

36

1 Superman
2 Captain Kirk
3 The Rover's Return
4 Julie Andrews
5 John Ford
6 Rorke's Drift
7 Kenneth More
8 Vittorio De Sica
9 *Star Wars* (1977)
10 Harrison Ford

63

1 Ulysses S. Grant
2 Al Jolson
3 Franklin Roosevelt
4 Dwight
5 Gerald Ford
6 Martin Luther King
7 William Pitt
8 Theodore Roosevelt
9 Alan Shepard
10 Henry Ford

90

1 Body-builder Charles Atlas
1 Wystan Hugh
3 Vasco da Gama
4 Bo Derek
5 Dennis Skinner
6 Mozart
7 Celtic and Liverpool
8 Billie Holiday
9 In a swimming accident
10 Scott

10   PEOPLE

1   Whom did Elzabeth Barrett marry?
2   Whose first hit record was 'These Arms of Mine'?
3   What instrument did Django Reinhardt play?
4   Who was Ehrich Weiss?
5   What do Americans do in a Howard Johnson?
6   What did Abebe Bikila do best?
7   Whose first novel was *Jigsaw*?
8   Who sang 'A Boy Named Sue'?
9   Who was Georges Escoffier?
10 What did Klaus Fuchs steal?

37   FILMS AND TV

1   Who played Batman in the 1989 film?
2   Who won an Oscar for his performance in *Rain Man*?
3   Who became the latest James Bond in *Licence to Kill*?
4   Who starred in *The Gold Rush*?
5   Who starred in *A Fistful of Dollars*?
6   Which actor starred in the 1970 film *Patton*?
7   Who did Frances Gumm become?
8   Which screen star was born Roy Scherer?
9   What was Gary Cooper's real first name?
10 Whom did Anna Neagle play in *Sixty Glorious Years*?

64   INVENTORS

1   Who invented the thermometer?
2   Who built a calculating machine in 1642?
3   Who made the first pendulum clock?
4   Who invented the lightning conductor?
5   Who invented bifocal glasses?
6   Who perfected the ballpoint pen?
7   Who made the first battery?
8   Who invented the dynamo?
9   What did Richard Trevithick pioneer?
10 What was a daguerreotype?

91   US PRESIDENTS

1   Who was the youngest elected US president?
2   Which president never married?
3   Who was the only president to resign his office?
4   Which US presidents were assassinated?
5   Which two presidents died on 4 July, 1826?
6   Who was the first president to broadcast on radio?
7   Who was the biggest president?
8   Who was chosen as President Bush's vice president?
9   Where was President Kennedy assassinated?
10 What was President Johnson's middle name?

10

1 Robert Browning
2 Otis Redding
3 Guitar
4 Houdini
5 Eat
6 Run marathons
7 Barbara Cartland
8 Johnny Cash
9 A famous chef
10 Atom secrets

37

1 Michael Keaton
2 Dustin Hoffman
3 Timothy Dalton
4 Charlie Chaplin
5 Clint Eastwood
6 George C Scott
7 Judy Garland
8 Rock Hudson
9 Frank
10 Queen Victoria

64

1 Galileo
2 Blaise Pascal
3 Christian Huygens
4 Benjamin Franklin
5 Benjamin Franklin
6 Laszlo Biro
7 Count Alessandro Volta
8 Faraday
9 Steam locomotive
10 An early form of photograph

91

1 John F. Kennedy
2 James Buchanan
3 Richard M. Nixon
4 Lincoln, Garfield, McKinley, Kennedy
5 Thomas Jefferson and John Adams
6 Woodrow Wilson
7 William H. Taft
8 Dan Quayle
9 Dallas
10 Baines

11 PEOPLE

1 Where did Hedda Hopper work?
2 What nationality is Melina Mercouri?
3 What did Willy Messerschmitt design?
4 What do the A.A. in A.A. Milne stand for?
5 What did the Mills Brothers do?
6 What was Margaret Mitchell's best-known book?
7 What is Mother Teresa's first given name?
8 Who is Sally Ride?
9 What was Pete Rose's game?
10 What kind of books did Tacitus write?

38 FILMS AND TV

1 Who played Glenn Miller and Charles Lindbergh on film?
2 Who played Tom Good in *The Good Life*?
3 Who commanded *The African Queen*?
4 Whose first film was *Steamboat Willie*?
5 Whose studio produced the *Keystone Kops* films?
6 Who played Guy Gibson in *The Dambusters*?
7 Who played Shane in the 1953 classic Western?
8 Who directed the film *The Alamo* (1960)?
9 Who made *Annie Hall* and *Manhattan*?
10 What was the subject of *A Bridge Too Far*?

65 INVENTORS

1 What did Samuel Colt make?
2 How did Walter Hunt keep things together?
3 What did Swan and Edison invent separately?
4 What did Robert Bunsen invent?
5 What was Melville Bissell's brainchild?
6 What did Lewis Waterman invent in 1884?
7 What did John Boyd Dunlop pioneer?
8 What did King C. Gillette develop?
9 What machine is associated with John P. Holland?
10 Who built the first man-carrying balloon?

92 US PRESIDENTS

1 Who was Ronald Reagan's vice president?
2 Which president was born at Lamar, Missouri in 1884?
3 What was President Coolidge's first name?
4 Which party did George Washington belong to?
5 What college did George Bush attend?
6 Which president was born at Tampico, Illinois in 1911?
7 Who was the first president to travel by railway train?
8 Which president had a grandfather who was president?
9 Where was President Johnson sworn in?
10 Which toy was supposedly named after a president?

A

11

1. Hollywood
2. Greek
3. Aeroplanes
4. Alan Alexander
5. Sing
6. *Gone With The Wind*
7. Agnes
8. An Astronaut
9. Baseball
10. History

38

1. James Stewart
2. Richard Briers
3. Humphrey Bogart
4. Walt Disney
5. Mack Sennett
6. Richard Todd
7. Alan Ladd
8. John Wayne
9. Woody Allen
10. The Arnhem campaign of 1944

65

1. Revolvers
2. With the improved safety pin (1849)
3. The electric light bulb
4. The bunsen burner
5. The carpet sweeper
6. The improved fountain pen
7. The pneumatic tyre
8. The safety razor
9. The submarine
10. The Montgolfier brothers

92

1. George Bush
2. Harry S. Truman
3. Calvin
4. None
5. Yale
6. Ronald Reagan
7. Andrew Jackson
8. Benjamin Harrison
9. On an aeroplane
10. Teddy bear (Theodore Roosevelt)

12 PEOPLE

1 Who was Marie Taglioni?
2 Who built the Menai suspension bridge?
3 Who climbed Mt Everest with Sir Edmund Hillary?
4 What did Eddy Merckx ride?
5 What nationality is Gary Player?
6 Who invented soda water?
7 Who composed *Peter and the Wolf*?
8 Who was Winston Churchill's mother?
9 Who invented Braille for the blind?
10 What did Leonid Brezhnev do in 1982?

39 FILMS AND TV

1 What nationality was Luis Buñuel?
2 Who directed *Les Enfants du Paradis*?
3 What nationality is Satyajit Ray?
4 Who directed *Lawrence of Arabia*?
5 Who starred in *Bad Day at Black Rock*?
6 Who wrote and starred in *A Fish Called Wanda*?
7 Who was the star of *Crocodile Dundee*?
8 Who was the star of *Coming to America*?
9 Who played Eliot Ness in the film *The Untouchables*?
10 Who were the stars of *Fatal Attraction*?

66 INVENTORS

1 What were Zeppelins?
2 What did Valdemar Poulsen pioneer?
3 What did Robert Watson-Watt develop in the 1930s?
4 What did John Logie Baird work on?
5 Who invented the atom-smasher or cyclotron?
6 What did Christopher Cockerell invent?
7 What did Wernher Von Braun send up?
8 Which British engineer pioneered jet engines?
9 How did Peter Goldmark make music last longer?
10 What was the Manhattan project?

93 US PRESIDENTS

1 Which president first spoke on TV?
2 Which president remained in office longest?
3 Who was the first president to live in the White House?
4 What was President Wilson's first name?
5 What was Richard Nixon's profession?
6 Who was the only Roman Catholic president?
7 To whom was Hubert Humphrey vice president?
8 Which president died aged 90 in 1964?
9 What is Ronald Reagan's middle name?
10 When did George Bush become president?

A

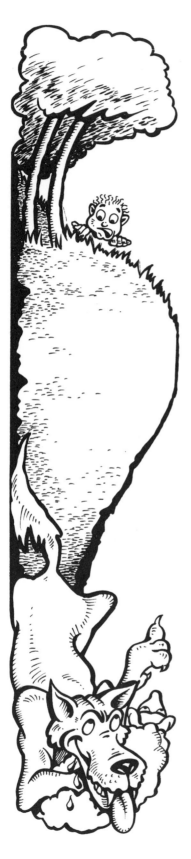

12

1 A ballerina
2 Thomas Telford
3 Tenzing Norgay
4 Bicycles
5 South African
6 Joseph Priestley
7 Prokofiev
8 Jennie Jerome
9 Louis Braille
10 Die

39

1 Spanish
2 Marcel Carne
3 Indian
4 David Lean
5 Spencer Tracy
6 John Cleese
7 Paul Hogan
8 Eddie Murphy
9 Kevin Costner
10 Glenn Close, Michael Douglas

66

1 Airships
2 Tape recording
3 Radar
4 Television
5 E.O. Lawrence
6 The hovercraft
7 Rockets
8 Sir Frank Whittle
9 He invented the LP record
10 The Allied atomic bomb project

93

1 Franklin D. Roosevelt
2 Franklin D. Roosevelt
3 John Adams
4 Woodrow
5 Lawyer
6 John F. Kennedy
7 Lyndon Johnson
8 Herbert Hoover
9 Wilson
10 1989

13 PLACES

1 Where is the Golden Gate Bridge?
2 Where is the Rialto Bridge?
3 Where is the Black Forest?
4 Where is the Ituri Forest?
5 Where is Edgbaston cricket ground?
6 Where is Old Trafford??
7 Where is the world's tallest skyscraper?
8 Where is the Raffles Hotel?
9 Where is Red Square?
10 Where is the home of the Mormon religion?

40 ASIA

1 Which country was formerly Siam?
2 Which country was part of Pakistan until 1971?
3 In which country is Ho Chi Minh City?
4 Which Asian country is now called Myanmar?
5 Which country's capital is Kabul?
6 Where is the Great Wall?
7 Where is Vientiane?
8 What is the capital of Sri Lanka?
9 What was Sri Lanka formerly called?
10 Where is Doha?

67 AUSTRALIA

1 What did the first Dutch explorers call Australia?
2 Where did Captain Cook land?
3 Who were the first Australians?
4 What arrived in Australia in 1788?
5 When is Australia Day?
6 Where did Matthew Flinder sail?
7 Where is Hobart?
8 Who was prime minister before Bob Hawke?
9 What is Australia's capital city?
10 What is the wild dog of Australia called?

94 PEOPLE

1 Which famous explorer was born in Genoa in 1451?
2 Where did Shakespeare die?
3 Where was Harun al-Raschid Caliph?
4 Where did Hannibal come from?
5 Whose mother's name was Schicklgruber?
6 Which saint was born at Domremy, France in 1412?
7 Where was Dr Johnson born?
8 Which county were Jack and Bobby Charlton born in?
9 Where is Daniel Arap Moi president?
10 In which country was Yehudi Menuhin born?

13

1 San Francisco
2 Venice
3 Germany
4 Zaire
5 Birmingham
6 Manchester
7 Chicago
8 Singapore
9 Moscow
10 Salt Lake City, USA

40

1 Thailand
2 Bangladesh
3 Vietnam
4 Burma
5 Afghanistan
6 China
7 Laos
8 Colombo
9 Ceylon
10 Qatar

67

1 New Holland
2 Botany Bay
3 The Aborigines
4 The first English settlement fleet
5 26 January
6 Round Australia
7 Tasmania
8 Malcolm Fraser
9 Canberra
10 Dingo

94

1 Christopher Columbus
2 Stratford
3 Baghdad
4 Carthage
5 Hitler
6 St Joan of Arc
7 Lichfield
8 County Durham
9 Kenya
10 United States

14 PLACES

1 Where is Lusaka?
2 Where is Casablanca?
3 Where is there a Battle of the Flowers?
4 Where does the Furry Dance take place?
5 Where is Ulan Bator?
6 Where is Qomolangma-feng?
7 Where is the world's largest inhabited castle?
8 Where is the world's tallest apartment block?
9 Where is the world's biggest stadium?
10 Where are the Promenade Concerts held?

41 ASIA

1 Which country has the world's biggest population?
2 On which island is Brunei?
3 Where are the ruins of Angkor Wat?
4 Of which country is Jakarta the capital?
5 Where are the Tigris and Euphrates rivers?
6 Of which country is Hussein king?
7 Where is Beirut?
8 What is Portugal's last colony in China?
9 Of which country is Kuala Lumpur the capital?
10 Which state is made up of 2,000 Indian Ocean islands?

68 AUSTRALIA

1 What was a bushranger?
2 What was Patrick White famous for?
3 Where is Australia's most famous opera house?
4 What sport did Newcombe and Roche excel at?
5 Who is Australia's most famous cricketer?
6 What is another name for the laughing jackass?
7 In which state is Melbourne?
8 How many Australian states are there?
9 Which is Australia's most famous rock?
10 Which is Australia's highest mountain?

95 PEOPLE

1 Which novelist helped design the R100 airship?
2 Who played Auntie Mame on Broadway and screen?
3 What is Pavarotti's first name?
4 Who was Rocco Francis Marchegiano?
5 What did Jean Claude Killy do downhill?
6 What did Ernst Heinkel design?
7 Whom did Jane Fonda marry in 1973?
8 What city was Bill Cosby born in?
9 Of which country was Benes a leader?
10 Who was the star of And God Created Woman (1956)?

A

14

1 Zambia
2 Morocco
3 Jersey
4 Helston, Cornwall
5 Mongolia
6 The Himalayas (Mt Everest)
7 Windsor
8 New York
9 Prague
10 Royal Albert Hall, London

41

1 China
2 Borneo
3 Cambodia
4 Indonesia
5 Iraq
6 Jordan
7 Lebanon
8 Macao
9 Malaysia
10 The Maldives

68

1 A highwayman or bandit
2 His writing
3 Sydney
4 Tennis
5 Sir Don Bradman
6 Kookaburra
7 Victoria
8 Six
9 Ayers Rock
10 Mt Kosciusko

95

1 Nevil Shute
2 Rosalind Russell
3 Luciano
4 Rocky Marciano
5 Ski
6 Aircraft
7 Tom Hayden
8 Philadelphia
9 Czechoslovakia
10 Brigitte Bardot

Q

15   PLACES

1 Where are the 'dreaming spires'?
2 Where is Tiger Bay?
3 Where is Princes Street?
4 Where is Phoenix Park?
5 Where in France is perfume-making a famous industry?
6 Where in Spain was famous for making swords?
7 Where in Spain did Gary Lineker play soccer?
8 Where is the Trooping the Colour ceremony staged?
9 Where are the British crown jewels kept?
10 Where is the world's tallest radio mast?

42   ASIA

1 Where is Damascus?
2 On which island is Nationalist China?
3 Of which country is Kathmandu the capital?
4 Where is Kai Tak airport?
5 Where is Calcutta?
6 Of which country is Tehran the capital?
7 Where is the Yellow River?
8 Which country besides Jordan borders the Dead Sea?
9 Of which country is Manila the capital?
10 Where is Kyoto?

69   AUSTRALIA

1 What money unit is used in Australia?
2 What is a mallee?
3 Which large lake in Australia is almost dry?
4 What is Australia's national flower?
5 Which Australian state is an island?
6 Which state covers the largest area?
7 Which state has Adelaide as its capital?
8 Where is Alice Springs?
9 What is the large gulf in northern Australia called?
10 In which state is Brisbane?

96   PEOPLE

1 What does the M in Richard M Nixon stand for?
2 Where did Matthew Henson go with Robert Peary?
3 What is Gregory Peck's full name?
4 Who wrote *The Four Just Men*?
5 What did the Great Wallendas do?
6 Who was Big Bill Tilden?
7 What did Marie Stopes pioneer?
8 What nationality was Lee Harvey Oswald's wife?
9 What was Eric Blair's pen name?
10 Who is Joanne Woodward's husband?

15

1 Oxford
2 Cardiff
3 Edinburgh
4 Dublin
5 Grasse
6 Toledo
7 Barcelona
8 Horse Guards Parade, London
9 Tower of London
10 Warsaw

42

1 Syria
2 Taiwan
3 Nepal
4 Hong Kong
5 India
6 Iran
7 China
8 Israel
9 The Philippines
10 Japan

69

1 Dollar
2 A small gum tree
3 Lake Eyre
4 Wattle
5 Tasmania
6 Western Australia
7 South Australia
8 In the Northern Territory
9 Gulf of Carpentaria
10 Queensland

96

1 Milhous
2 The North Pole in 1909
3 Gregory Eldred Peck
4 Edgar Wallace
5 They were circus performers
6 A US tennis star of the 1920s
7 Birth control
8 Russian
9 George Orwell
10 Paul Newman

16 PLACES

1 Where do Mancunians come from?
2 Which is the main river of Nottinghamshire?
3 In which English county is Buxton?
4 Which city is also known as the Potteries?
5 Which was London's main airport before Heathrow?
6 In which English county is Devizes?
7 Where is the Ashmolean Museum?
8 Which Scottish city is called the Granite City?
9 What breakfast food is associated with Dundee?
10 On which river does Liverpool stand?

43 HISTORY

1 Who sat beneath a Bo tree?
2 Who led the Peasants' Revolt of 1381?
3 Whose was the 'Greatest Show on Earth'?
4 Who went with Burton in search of the source of the Nile?
5 Who founded Methodism?
6 Who sailed to India in 1497?
7 Who pioneered holiday camps in Britain?
8 Who wrote *Robinson Crusoe*?
9 Who was prime minister before Mrs Thatcher?
10 Which jockey was knighted in 1953?

70 STORY TELLERS

1 Who wrote the thriller *Freaky Deaky*?
2 In Greek myth, who fell in love with his reflection?
3 Who wrote a novel about a white whale?
4 What was the novel's title?
5 Who wrote *Treasure Island*?
6 In which of Dickens' novels does Sam Weller appear?
7 Who wrote *The Murders in the Rue Morgue*?
8 Who wrote *The Just So Stories*?
9 Who wrote the *War of the Worlds*?
10 Who wrote *Animal Farm*?

97 PLACES

1 Where would you ride on a footplate?
2 Which house is famous for a racket sport and horse trials?
3 Where is St Cuthbert's tomb?
4 Where do blue gums grow?
5 On which river does Quebec stand?
6 Where is the Grand Canal?
7 Where is the Whispering Gallery?
8 Where is Churchill buried?
9 Where are the Elgin Marbles kept?
10 Which country has the most crowded trains?

A

16

1 Manchester
2 Trent
3 Derbyshire
4 Stoke-on-Trent
5 Croydon
6 Wiltshire
7 Oxford
8 Abderdeen
9 Marmalade
10 The river Mersey

43

1 Buddha
2 Wat Tyler
3 Barnum and Bailey's
4 John Hanning Speke
5 Charles and John Wesley
6 Vasco da Gama
7 Billy Butlin
8 Daniel Defoe
9 James Callaghan
10 Gordon Richards

70

1 Elmore Leonard
2 Narcissus
3 Herman Melville
4 *Moby Dick*
5 Robert Louis Stevenson
6 *Pickwick Papers*
7 Edgar Allan Poe
8 Rudyard Kipling
9 H.G. Wells
10 George Orwell

97

1 On a steam locomotive
2 Badminton
3 Durham Cathedral
4 Australia
5 St Lawrence
6 Venice
7 St Paul's Cathedral
8 Bladon in Oxfordshire
9 The British Museum
10 Japan

17   PLACES

1 Which is the most northerly county in England?
2 Where do scouses come from?
3 Which is the largest city in Wales?
4 Which is the largest city in Northern Ireland?
5 Which county is called the Garden of England?
6 Which is England's highest mountain?
7 Which county is it in?
8 Where is the Forest of Dean?
9 In which mountain range is Aviemore?
10 On which river does Glasgow stand?

44   HISTORY

1 Who led the Mormons across the Great Salt Lake?
2 For what was Cicero famous?
3 Who built the *Rocket* steam locomotive?
4 Who was the most famous director of the Russian Ballet?
5 For what was Casanova famous?
6 Who was called The Scourge of God?
7 Who was Alexander Selkirk?
8 Who founded the Chinese Republic?
9 Who was the first Tudor monarch?
10 Which English poet fought for the Dutch in 1586?

71   STORY TELLERS

1 Which Greek hero slew Hector of Troy?
2 What is the name of Robin Hood's fat friar?
3 Which Brontë sister wrote *Wuthering Heights*?
4 Who wrote *The Count of Monte Cristo*?
5 What was Lewis Carroll's real name?
6 What was Winnie the Pooh's favourite food?
7 Who wrote about hobbits?
9 What kind of animal is Babar in the children's stories?
9 Who is the boy hero of the *The Jungle Books*?
10 In which Dickens novel does Scrooge appear?

98   PLACES

1 Where would you find a kibbutz?
2 What industry was Kidderminster famous for?
3 Where is the Milford Track?
4 What is the Nameless Tower of Trango?
5 Where is New Caledonia?
6 Whereabouts in England is Holland?
7 In which county is Ironbridge?
8 In which island group is Iona?
9 Where are the Murchison Falls?
10 Where are the Shalimar Gardens?

A

17

1 Northumberland
2 Liverpool
3 Cardiff
4 Belfast
5 Kent
6 Scafell Pike
7 Cumbria
8 Gloucestershire
9 The Cairngorms
10 The river Clyde

44

1 Brigham Young
2 Oratory
3 George Stephenson
4 Diaghilev
5 His love affairs
6 Attila the Hun
7 The real-life Robinson Crusoe
8 Sun Yat Sen
9 Henry VII
10 Sir Philip Sidney

71

1 Achilles
2 Friar Tuck
3 Emily
4 Alexandre Dumas
5 Charles Luttwidge Dodgson
6 Honey
7 J.R.R. Tolkien
8 Elephant
9 Mowgli
10 *A Christmas Carol*

98

1 Israel
2 Carpets
3 New Zealand
4 A rock climb in Pakistan
5 The Pacific
6 Lincolnshire
7 Shropshire
8 Inner Hebrides
9 Uganda
10 Lahore, Pakistan

18 PLACES

1 To which island group does Skye belong?
2 Where is Muckle Flugga?
3 Which is the longest river in Northern Ireland?
4 In which county is Land's End?
5 Which is the biggest lake in the British Isles?
6 On which river does Dublin stand?
7 What is the highest point in Ireland?
8 Where is St Colman's Cathedral?
9 What is the Welsh name for Swansea?
10 In which English county is Bracknell?

45 HISTORY

1 Who said 'The ballot is stronger than the bullet'?
2 Who was Kwame Nkrumah?
3 Who was Britain's first Poet Laureate?
4 Which queen married Lord Darnley?
5 Of which country is Lieutenant General Suharto president?
6 Which leader nationalized the Suez Canal in 1956?
7 Who led the Cuban revolution in 1959?
8 Which British prime minister met Hitler in Munich?
9 What was General De Gaulle's first name?
10 Who is President of Egypt?

72 STORY TELLERS

1 Who was the one-legged pirate in *Treasure Island*?
2 Who sailed with Jason to find the Golden Fleece?
3 Who wrote *The Thirty Nine Steps*?
4 Who created George Smiley?
5 Who wrote the James Bond Books?
6 In which book do the people of Lilliput appear?
7 Who created Winnie the Pooh?
8 Which animal fell asleep at the Mad Hatter's party?
9 Who created Tom Sawyer and Huckleberry Finn?
10 What was this author's real name?

99 EUROPE

1 Where does the Grimaldi family rule?
2 What is another name for Brugge?
3 On which river does Brussels stand?
4 Which country is known locally as Hellas or Ellas?
5 Where is Linz?
6 In which country is Hochstadt?
7 On which Channel Island is Saint Peter Port?
8 In which range of mountains is Mt Narodnaya?
9 Which country has a province and port named Burgas?
10 Which capital city was once called Christiana?

18

1 Hebrides
2 The Shetland Isles
3 The river Bann
4 Cornwall
5 Lough Neagh
6 The river Liffey
7 Carrauntoohill
8 Cobh
9 Abertawe
10 Berkshire

45

1 Abraham Lincoln
2 First prime minister of Ghana
3 John Dryden
4 Mary Queen of Scots
5 Indonesia
6 Gamal Abdel Nasser
7 Fidel Castro
8 Neville Chamberlain
9 Charles
10 Hosni Mubarak

72

1 Long John Silver
2 The Argonauts
3 John Buchan
4 John Le Carré
5 Ian Fleming
6 *Gulliver's Travels*
7 A.A. Milne
8 The Dormouse
9 Mark Twain
10 Samuel Langhorne Clemens

99

1 Monaco
2 Bruges
3 Senne
4 Greece
5 Austria
6 Germany
7 Guernsey
8 Urals
9 Bulgaria
10 Oslo

19   SPORT

1 In what year did Muhammad Ali win his first world title?
2 In what year was Ian Botham born?
3 What nationality is Jack Brabham?
4 Who averaged 99.94 in Test cricket?
5 Which soccer club did Matt Busby manage?
6 What sport did Donald Budge play?
7 What is Sebastian Coe's middle name?
8 How many players are there in a Rugby League team?
9 Who was known as the Manassa Mauler?
10 For which club did Di Stefano play soccer?

46   HISTORY

1 Who resigned over Henry VIII's divorce?
2 Who took Christianity to Japan?
3 Whom did Elizabeth I succeed?
4 Who sailed round the world in 1577-80?
5 Which country did Boris Godunov rule?
6 Where did Tokugawa Ieyasu rule?
7 Where did Samuel de Champlain explore?
8 What did Guy Fawkes and his friends try to blow up?
9 Who was Queen Henrietta Maria?
10 Who suceeded Oliver Cromwell?

73   STORY TELLERS

1 Which horror character did Bram Stoker create?
2 Who wrote a poem about an owl and a pussycat?
3 What did the ugly duckling grow up to be?
4 Where was Eric Williams' book *The Wooden Horse* set?
5 Where did the Wizard of Oz live?
6 Which children's favourite lives in Nutwood?
7 What sport does Dick Francis write about?
8 What kind of books does P. D. James write?
9 Who wrote *On the Road*?
10 Who wrote *Dune*?

100   THE GREAT AND NOT SO GREAT

1 Which missionary discovered Victoria Falls?
2 Who founded the Society of Friends?
3 What did Wiley Post do in 1933?
4 What is French President Mitterrand's first name?
5 Where was Errol Flynn born?
6 Who was Larry Hagman's mother?
7 In which US city was Madonna born?
8 By what name is Reg Dwight more commonly known?
9 What was Hitler's artistic ambition?
10 Who was Joseph Smith?

19

1　1964
2　1955
3　Australian
4　Don Bradman
5　Manchester United
6　Tennis
7　Newbold
8　13
9　Jack Dempsey
10　Real Madrid

46

1　Sir Thomas More
2　St Francis Xavier
3　Mary I
4　Sir Francis Drake
5　Russia
6　Japan
7　Canada
8　The Houses of Parliament
9　The wife of Charles I
10　His son Richard

73

1　Dracula
2　Edward Lear
3　A swan
4　A POW camp in Germany
5　The Emerald City
6　Rupert Bear
7　Horse racing
8　Detective stories
9　Jack Kerouac
10　Frank Herbert

100

1　David Livingstone
2　George Fox
3　Flew solo round the world
4　François
5　Tasmania
6　Mary Martin
7　Detroit
8　Elton John
9　He wanted to be a painter
10　The Founder of the Mormon Church

Q

20   SPORT

1   What sport did Joe DiMaggio play?
2   What do the W.G. in W.G. Grace stand for?
3   Where will the 1992 Olympic Games be held?
4   Which countries compete for the Calcutta Cup?
5   What was Billie-Jean King's single name?
6   What nationality was racing driver Niki Lauda?
7   In which sport do people win Lonsdale Belts?
8   Which sportsman was called the Brown Bomber?
9   For which country does Paul Thorburn play rugby?
10 Who is nicknamed the 'Golden Bear'?

47   HISTORY

1   Which British king fled to France in 1688?
2   Which king was known as the Sun King?
3   Who led his troops to victory at Blenheim?
4   Which country was ruled by Frederick the Great?
5   Who was the Young Pretender?
6   Who won the Battle of the Pyramids in 1798?
7   Where did Robert Clive extend British power?
8   Where did General Wolfe die?
9   Who commanded the Americans in the Revolutionary War?
10 Who surrendered at Yorktown in 1781?

74   STORY TELLERS

1   Who wrote *I Claudius*?
2   Who was Dr Watson's more perceptive companion?
3   What was Molière's real name?
4   Which novelist's real name was Mary Ann Evans?
5   Father and son, Kingsley and Martin ...who?
6   Who wrote *The Great Gatsby*?
7   What nationality was Thomas Mann?
8   Who wrote *The Call of the Wild*?
9   Which poet wrote *A Shropshire Lad*?
10 Who wrote *Brideshead Revisited*?

101   THE GREAT AND NOT SO GREAT

1   Who played James Bond in *Licensed to Kill*?
2   What newspaper was owned by Lord Beaverbrook?
3   Which US president was not elected?
4   Who was the first vicar of the Christian Church?
5   What is the present Pope's country of birth?
6   What did Alexander the Great die of?
7   Who is the patron saint of Wales?
8   How did Dr Crippen achieve notoriety?
9   Who invented the miner's safety lamp?
10 Which US President was assassinated in 1881?

A

20

1. Baseball
2. William Gilbert
3. Barcelona
4. England and Scotland (Rugby Union)
5. Moffat
6. Austrian
7. Boxing
8. Joe Louis
9. Wales
10. Jack Nicklaus

47

1. James II
2. Louix XI
3. The Duke of Marlborough
4. Prussia
5. Bonnie Prince Charlie
6. Napoleon
7. India
8. Quebec
9. George Washington
10. The British under Cornwallis

74

1. Robert Graves
2. Sherlock Holmes
3. Jean Baptiste Poquelin
4. George Eliot
5. Amis
6. F. Scott Fitzgerald
7. German
8. Jack London
9. A.E. Housman
10. Evelyn Waugh

101

1. Timothy Dalton
2. The *Daily Express*
3. Gerald Ford
4. St Peter
5. Poland
6. Fever and exhaustion
7. St David
8. He was a murderer
9. Humphry Davy
10. Garfield

Q

21   *SPORT*

1 In what country was Ilie Nastase born?
2 What game was devised by James Naismith?
3 Who lost three Wimbledon finals in 1977?
4 In which sport is the Jules Rimet Trophy awarded?
5 Which British tennis player won Wimbledon in 1977?
6 Which county did Fred Trueman play cricket for?
7 Which football club plays at Ibrox?
8 In what year did Sebastian Coe set three world records?
9 What was Gary Sobers' first name in full?
10 In which sport is Jahangir Khan a star?

48   *HISTORY*

1 Where did Gustavus Adolphus rule?
2 Which Scottish clan was slaughtered at Glencoe?
3 What happened to Louis XVI and his wife?
4 Who were Danton and Robespierre?
5 Who mutinied in 1797 at Spithead?
6 What year did the Jacobite's lose the battle of Culloden?
7 Where did Lewis and Clark explore?
8 Who crowned Napoleon emperor of France?
9 Which sea battle was fought in October 1805?
10 Where did Admiral Nelson die?

75   *STORY TELLERS*

1 Who created Dr Watson?
2 Where did Phileas Fogg travel?
3 In which Dickens novel does the Artful Dodger appear?
4 Where does Toad live, in *Wind in the Willows*?
5 What were T.S.Eliot's first names?
6 Who wrote *The Pit and the Pendulum*?
7 What kind of books is Louis L'Amour famous for?
8 What post did Wordsworth and Tennyson each hold?
9 Whose life did Boswell write?
10 Who wrote *Ivanhoe*?

102   *THE GREAT AND NOT SO GREAT*

1 Who is the patron saint of Ireland?
2 Who popularized the saying 'Go West, young man'?
3 What was St Paul's name before his conversion?
4 Who was Henry O. Flipper?
5 What nationality was Sigmund Freud?
6 With what was Dorothea Beale concerned?
7 Who introduced the Christmas tree to Great Britain?
8 Who was the first Christian martyr?
9 How did J. J. Astor make his millions?
10 What organization did Henri Dunant found?

A

21

1 Romania
2 Basketball
3 Betty Stöve
4 Football
5 Virginia Wade
6 Yorkshire
7 Glasgow Rangers
8 1981
9 Garfield
10 Squash

48

1 Sweden
2 The Macdonalds
3 They were executed in 1793
4 Leaders of the French revolution
5 British sailors
6 1745
7 North America
8 He crowned himself
9 The Battle of Trafalgar
10 On board HMS *Victory*

75

1 Sir Arthur Conan Doyle
2 *Around the World in 80 Days*
3 *Oliver Twist*
4 Toad Hall
5 Thomas Stearns
6 Edgar Allan Poe
7 Westerns
8 Poet Laureate
9 Samuel Johnson
10 Sir Walter Scott

102

1 St Patrick
2 Horace Greeley
3 Saul
4 First black graduate from West Point
5 Austrian
6 Girls' education
7 Prince Albert
8 St Stephen
9 In furs, banks, property
10 The Red Cross

22   EUROPE

1 Which is Europe's biggest lake?
2 Which two countries share the Matterhorn?
3 How much of Europe is officially desert?
4 Where is Vichy?
5 Where is a famous Passion Play held?
6 How many countries make up the continent of Europe?
7 Which famous composer was born in Bonn?
8 Which is Europe's longest river?
9 What was the former name for the Ijsselmeer?
10 Which European country produces 'green' wine?

49   HISTORY

1 What barrier went up in 1961?
2 What were made legal in Great Britain in 1871?
3 Who was Charles Stewart Parnell?
4 Who became Britain's king in 1910?
5 What organization was set up in May 1945?
6 Which sea disaster occurred in 1912?
7 Who received Marshall Aid?
8 Which African country is led by Robert Mugabe?
9 Who took over from Lenin as leader of the USSR in 1924?
10 What year was Britain's general strike?

76   WHERE IS...?

1 Where is Basra?
2 Where is Amman?
3 Where is Istanbul?
4 Where is Gdansk?
5 Where is Karachi?
6 Where is the Golden Temple of Amritsar?
7 Where is Managua?
8 Where is Tianamen Square?
9 Where are the UN headquarters?
10 Where is Mecca?

103   PLACES

1 Is Alsager a town in England, Norway or Sweden?
2 Where are the Babine Mountains?
3 Who discovered the Bering Strait in 1728?
4 By what name is Mt Godwin Austen better known?
5 Is Kalamazoo a place in the USA, Nigeria or China?
6 Which is the longest river in France?
7 In which US city is Coney Island?
8 Which city is known to its citizens as Beograd?
9 Where is the Gibson Desert?
10 Who fought whom on the Plains of Abraham in 1759?

A

22

1 Lake Ladoga
2 Italy and Switzerland
3 None
4 France
5 Oberammergau
6 34
7 Beethoven
8 The Volga
9 The Zuider Zee
10 Portugal

49

1 The Berlin Wall
2 Trade unions
3 An Irish MP and nationalist
4 Edward VII
5 The United Nations
6 The liner Titanic sank
7 European nations, to rebuild after
   World War II
8 Zimbabwe
9 Stalin
10 1926

76

1 Iraq
2 Jordan
3 Turkey
4 Poland
5 Pakistan
6 India
7 Nicaragua
8 Peking
9 New York
10 Saudi Arabia

103

1 England
2 British Columbia, Canada
3 Vitus Bering
4 K2
5 USA
6 Loire
7 New York
8 Belgrade
9 Australia
10 The British defeated the French

23 *EUROPE*

1 Which country includes Zeeland and Bornholm islands?
2 Which is farthest south: Toulouse or Venice?
3 Which sea is the port of Odessa on?
4 Which river flows through Warsaw?
5 Is Spain bigger or smaller than France?
6 Where is the language Romansh spoken?
7 Which countries border Liechtenstein?
8 What is the capital of Switzerland?
9 To whom do the Faeroe Islands belong?
10 Which European state has an area of 0.44 sq km?

50 *HISTORY*

1 Who succeeded Edward VIII after his abdication?
2 When did World War II begin?
3 When did the USA enter the war?
4 What event brought the USA into the war?
5 Which country captured Port Arthur in 1905?
6 What year did Ireland join the European Community?
7 Where was Archduke Franz Ferdinand of Austria shot dead?
8 Where were war crimes trials held from 1945 to 1947?
9 What do the letters ANC stand for?
10 Who led Britain's post-war Labour government?

77 *WHERE IS...?*

1 Where is Panmunjon?
2 Where was Checkpoint Charlie?
3 What was the capital of South Vietnam?
4 Where is Vilnius?
5 Where is Havana?
6 Where did the Tontons Macoutes operate?
7 Where is Tripoli?
8 Where is Sofia?
9 Where is Tirane?
10 Where did Hitler die?

104 *PLACES*

1 Where is the world's oldest parliament?
2 Which London Tube line is coloured green on the map?
3 Which British city has Piccadilly and Victoria rail stations?
4 What is the Bay of Fundy famous for?
5 Which sea has the clearest water?
6 Which desert has the highest sand dunes?
7 Where and when was Britain's longest drought?
8 Where was the Cullinan diamond found?
9 Where is the oldest astronomical observatory?
10 Where is Bamako?

A

23

1   Denmark
2   Toulouse
3   The Black Sea
4   The Vistula
5   Smaller
6   Switzerland
7   Austria and Switzerland
8   Bern
9   Denmark
10 The Vatican City

50

1   George VI
2   September 3, 1939
3   December 8, 1941
4   Japan's attack on Pearl Harbor
5   Japan
6   1973
7   Sarajevo
8   Nuremberg
9   African National Congress
10 Clement Attlee

77

1   Korea
2   Berlin
3   Saigon
4   Lithuania
5   Cuba
6   Haiti
7   Libya
8   Bulgaria
9   Albania
10 Berlin

104

1   The Althing, Iceland
2   District Line
3   Manchester
4   High tides
5   Weddell Sea in Antarctica
6   Sahara
7   (1893) London
8   South Africa
9   Athens (Tower of the Winds)
10 Mali

24   EUROPE

1 In which city is the Karntnerstrasse?
2 What is the capital of Belgium?
3 Where do people speak Manx?
4 Where is Thessaly?
5 What is the Icelandic for Iceland?
6 Which country's name means 'the road to the north'?
7 Where is Serbo-Croat an official language?
8 What currency is used in San Marino?
9 On which river does Florence stand?
10 Where is the Dingle Peninsula?

51   HISTORY

1 What barrier went up in 1961?
2 Who was Archbishop Makarios?
3 Where is the Bay of Pigs?
4 What post did U Thant hold?
5 When was the Six Day War?
6 How many atom bombs were dropped on Japan?
7 Which European dictator died in 1975?
8 What was the only major sea battle of World War I?
9 What year did Elizabeth II become queen?
10 What happened on August 2 1990?

78   WHERE IS...?

1 Where is Mogadishu?
2 Which island is split between Greek and Turkish groups?
3 Which country left the Commonwealth in 1961?
4 Where is Port Stanley?
5 Where is Monrovia?
6 In which country did the 'Prague Spring' take place?
7 Where is Uzbekistan?
8 Where is Riga?
9 What is the capital of Grenada?
10 Where is Windhoek?

105   PLACES

1 Where is Pondichery?
2 Which US city was once called Yerba Buena?
3 Which Asian country has Gangtok as its capital?
4 To which island group does Tahiti belong?
5 Where are Sodom and Gomorrah today?
6 Which US state is the First State?
7 Is Kanchenjunga a river, a lake or a mountain?
8 In which European country is Bergen?
9 Which royal residence is in Norfolk?
10 In which continent is Suriname?

A

24

1 Vienna
2 Brussels
3 The Isle of Man
4 Greece
5 Island
6 Norway
7 Yugoslavia
8 The lira
9 The Arno
10 Ireland

51

1 South Africa
2 First president of Cyprus
3 Cuba
4 UN secretary general
5 1967
6 Two
7 Francisco Franco
8 Battle of Jutland
9 1952
10 Iraq invaded Kuwait

78

1 Somalia
2 Cyprus
3 South Africa
4 The Falklands
5 Liberia
6 Czechoslovakia
7 The USSR
8 Latvia
9 St George's
10 Namibia

105

1 India
2 San Francisco
3 Sikkim
4 Society Islands
5 Possibly under the Dead Sea
6 Delaware
7 Mountain
8 Norway
9 Sandringham
10 South America

25 WHO WERE THEY?

1 What nationality was Prince Henry the Navigator?
2 Who commanded HMS *Bounty* in 1787?
3 Which German leader was called the Iron Chancellor?
4 Who was the first person to cross the Channel by aeroplane?
5 Which country did Ivan the Terrible rule?
6 Who was the first woman MP?
7 Who was King Arthur's father?
8 What was Marshal Tito's real name?
9 Who was Adolf Hitler's mistress?
10 Who was the first Christian emperor of Rome?

52 CAN YOU NAME...?

1 The world's highest mountain?
2 The driest desert in South America?
3 The longest river?
4 The world's largest volcano?
5 The longest river in North America?
6 The river also known as the Zaire?
7 The ocean with the deepest water?
8 The longest gorge?
9 The deepest gorge?
10 The world's highest lake?

79 THE BIBLE

1 Which is the first book of the Bible?
2 Which is the first book of the New Testament?
3 Which is the last book of the Bible?
4 How many books make up the Pentateuch?
5 What does the word *Apocrypha* mean?
6 When did the first English Bible appear?
7 Which Bible was printed in 1611 in England?
8 Which part of the Bible do Jews accept?
9 How many books are there in the Protestant Bible?
10 What was Luke's profession?

106 THE ARTS

1 What is the name of King Lear's youngest daughter?
2 Who wrote *The Doctor's Dilemma* and *Pygmalion*?
3 Who composed the *Hungarian Rhapsodies*?
4 Who backed Kid Creole?
5 With which band does Jerry Garcia play?
6 Who began the Promenade Concerts in London?
7 What nationality was Sibelius?
8 How does the Duke of Clarence die in *Richard III*?
9 Who painted the ceiling of the Sistine Chapel?
10 Who was Hamlet's stepfather?

A

25

1. Portuguese
2. Captain Bligh
3. Bismarck
4. Louis Blériot
5. Russia
6. Nancy Astor
7. Uther Pendragon
8. Josip Broz
9. Eva Braun
10. Constantine

52

1. Mt Everest
2. The Atacama Desert
3. The Nile
4. Mauna Loa
5. Mississippi-Missouri
6. The Congo
7. The Pacific Ocean
8. Grand Canyon
9. Hells Canyon
10. Lake Titicaca

79

1. Genesis
2. Matthew
3. John
4. Five
5. Hidden (Greek)
6. Around 1380
7. King James Version
8. Old Testament
9. 66
10. He was a doctor

106

1. Cordelia
2. Shaw
3. Liszt
4. The Coconuts
5. Grateful Dead
6. Sir Henry Wood
7. Finnish
8. He drowns in malmsey wine
9. Michelangelo
10. Claudius

Q

26 *WHO WERE THEY?*

1 Which English king had six wives?
2 Who was the second president of the United States?
3 Who succeeded Lord Carrington as foreign secretary?
4 Who had a horse called Bucephalus?
5 Who was the last English king named George?
6 Which famous British soldier was killed at Khartoum?
7 Who was shot dead by Robert Ford in 1882?
8 Who told the workers of the world to unite?
9 Who was Grandma Moses?
10 Who was called the 'King of Swing'?

53 *CAN YOU NAME...?*

1 The largest lake in the world?
2 The deepest lake in the world?
3 The biggest ocean?
4 The biggest desert?
5 The biggest desert in Asia?
6 The largest lake in North America?
7 The highest waterfall?
8 The waterfall with the most water?
9 The longest Australian river?
10 The highest mountain range completely in Europe?

80 *THE BIBLE*

1 Who were Adam and Eve's sons?
2 Where did Abraham travel?
3 Who wore a coat of many colours?
4 Who was thrown into the lions' den?
5 Who seduced Samson?
6 Who killed Goliath?
7 What weapon did he use?
8 Who were Isaac's sons?
9 Who was swallowed by a whale?
10 Who were the sons of Noah?

107 *THE ARTS*

1 Who composed the *Minute Waltz*?
2 What was Van Gogh's first name?
3 Who had a UK chart topper with 'Distant Drums' (1966)?
4 Who wrote the music for *The Sound of Music*?
5 Who painted the *Mona Lisa*?
6 Who wrote the song 'Mad Dogs and Englishmen'?
7 What is the title of Beethoven's only opera?
8 Where was Dave Edmunds born?
9 What kind of music did Scott Joplin play?
10 Where does the Syracuse Symphony Orchestra come from?

26

1　Henry VIII
2　John Adams
3　Francis Pym
4　Alexander the Great
5　George VI
6　General Gordon
7　Jesse James
8　Karl Marx
9　An American painter
10　Benny Goodman

53

1　The Caspian Sea
2　Lake Baikal
3　The Pacific Ocean
4　The Sahara Desert
5　The Arabian Desert
6　Lake Superior
7　Angel Falls
8　Niagara Falls
9　Darling River
10　The Alps

80

1　Cain and Abel
2　From Ur to Canaan
3　Joseph
4　Daniel
5　Delilah
6　David
7　Slingshot
8　Jacob and Esau
9　Jonah
10　Shem, Ham, Japheth

107

1　Chopin
2　Vincent
3　Jim Reeves
4　Richard Rodgers
5　Leonardo da Vinci
6　Noel Coward
7　*Fidelio*
8　Cardiff
9　Ragtime
10　USA

Q

27 WHO WERE THEY?

1 Who was Christopher Robin's real-life father?
2 Who was Elvis Presley's manager?
3 Who founded the Pulitzer prizes?
4 Who led the slaves' revolt in Rome?
5 Who lost the Battle of the Little Bighorn?
6 Who took the first step on the Moon?
7 Who was the first Holy Roman Emperor?
8 Who wrote *The Ugly Duckling*?
9 Who was the only king of England called 'Great'?
10 Who scored a hat-trick in the 1966 World Cup Final?

54 CAN YOU NAME...?

1 The highest peak in Europe?
2 The highest mountain in North America?
3 The largest lake in South America?
4 The Spanish word describing the South American plains?
5 Antarctica's greatest active volcano?
6 The highest mountain range in North Africa?
7 Africa's greatest waterfall?
8 A South African fall, second highest in the world?
9 The waterway that joins the Mediterranean and Red Sea?
10 The world's longest lake?

81 THE BIBLE

1 Who was St Peter's brother?
2 How many disciples did Jesus originally choose?
3 Who was the youngest apostle?
4 Who betrayed Jesus?
5 Who was raised from the dead by Jesus?
6 Who first saw Jesus after his resurrection?
7 Who wrote the second Gospel?
8 Which apostle was a tax collector?
9 Which apostle wrote letters to the early Churches?
10 Who was Silas?

108 THE ARTS

1 Who composed the opera *I Pagliacci*?
2 What instrument did Charlie Parker play?
3 What was Fats Waller's real first name?
4 Who had a 1979 hit with 'Bad Girls'?
5 With which band did David Byrne make a name?
6 Who wrote the epic poem *Paradise Lost*?
7 How many people attended Mozart's funeral?
8 In which language did Dante write?
9 In which Shakespeare play does Malvolio appear?
10 How many people made up the original Style Council?

A

27

1 A.A. Milne
2 Colonel Parker
3 Joseph Pulitzer
4 Spartacus
5 General George Custer
6 Neil Armstrong
7 Charlemagne
8 Hans Christian Andersen
9 Alfred
10 Geoff Hurst

54

1 Mt Elbrus
2 Mt McKinley
3 Lake Maracaibo
4 Pampas
5 Mt Erebus
6 Atlas Mts
7 Victoria Falls
8 Tugela Falls
9 The Suez Canal
10 Lake Tanganyika

81

1 Andrew
2 12
3 Revelation
4 Judas Iscariot
5 Lazarus
6 Mary Magdalene
7 Mark
8 Matthew
9 Paul
10 One of Paul's companions

108

1 Ruggiero Leoncavallo
2 Alto saxophone
3 Thomas
4 Donna Summer
5 Talking Heads
6 John Milton
7 One
8 Italian
9 *Twelfth Night*
10 Two

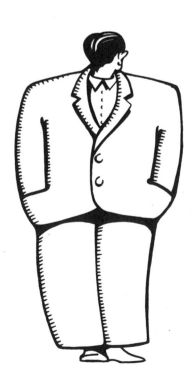